**THE BRITISH MUSEUM** Pocket Dictionary

# ANCIENT EGYPTIAN
# GODS & GODDESSES

## George Hart

THE BRITISH MUSEUM PRESS

First published in 2001 by
The British Museum Press
A division of The British Museum Company Ltd
38 Russell Square, London WC1B 3QQ

Reprinted 2003, 2006, 2007, 2011, 2013

ISBN 978-0-7141-1948-9

George Hart has asserted the right to be
identified as the author of this work.

A catalogue record for this title is available
from the British Library.

Designed and typeset by
HERRING BONE DESIGN
Hieroglyphs typeset by Nigel Strudwick using
the Cleo Font designed by Cleo Huggins.

Printed in Malaysia by Tien Wah Press

# CONTENTS

A-Z Index of
Gods & Goddesses  4

## CREATOR GODS &GODDESSES

Atum  5

Khepry  6

Re-Horakhty  7

Shu and Tefnut  8

Geb and Nut  9

Ptah  10

Apis Bull  11

Khnum  12

## THE GREAT GODDESSES

Bastet  13

Hathor  14

Sekhmet  15

Neith  16

Selqet  17

The Two
Ladies  18

## DEITIES OF THEBES

Amun 20

Mut 21

Khonsu 22

Aten 23

Montu 24

## GODS, GODDESSES & KINGSHIP

Isis  25

Nephthys  27

Horus  28

Seth  30

Pharaoh  31

Wepwawet  32

## DEITIES OF DEATH & THE UNDERWORLD

Underworld Deities 33

Osiris 34

Anubis 36

The Sons of Horus 37

Assessor Gods 38

Ammut 39

Apophis 40

## GODS & GODDESSES OF DAILY LIFE

Bes  41

Hapy  42

Sobek  43

Taweret  44

Thoth  45

Maat  46

Imhotep  47

## AN INVENTED GOD

Sarapis 48

# A–Z Index of Gods and Goddesses

| | | | | | |
|---|---|---|---|---|---|
| Ammut | 39 | Isis | 25 | Re | 7 |
| Amun | 20 | | | | |
| Anubis | 36 | Khepry | 6 | Sekhmet | 15 |
| Apis Bull | 11 | Khnum | 12 | Sarapis | 48 |
| Apophis | 40 | Khonsu | 22 | Selqet | 17 |
| Assessor | | | | Seth | 30 |
| Gods | 38 | Maat | 46 | Shu | 8 |
| Aten | 23 | Montu | 24 | Sobek | 43 |
| Atum | 5 | Mut | 21 | Sons of Horus | |
| | | | | | 37 |
| Bastet | 13 | Neith | 16 | Taweret | 44 |
| Bes | 41 | Nekhbet | 18 | Tefnut | 8 |
| | | Nephthys | 27 | Thoth | 45 |
| Geb | 9 | Nut | 9 | Two Ladies | 18 |
| Hapy | 42 | Osiris | 34 | Wadjyt | 18 |
| Hathor | 14 | | | Wepwawet | 32 |
| Horus | 28 | Pharaoh | 31 | | |
| | | Ptah | 10 | Underworld | |
| Imhotep | 47 | | | Deities | 33 |

# ATUM

Atum is a form of the sun-god. He is described as the all-powerful 'Lord to the limits of the sky' and he wears the clothes and regalia of a pharaoh. Sometimes he symbolizes the sun setting on the western horizon.

A gold pectoral (an ornament worn on the chest) depicting Atum (on the left) wearing a royal kilt and the Double Crown of Upper and Lower Egypt.

Before the world existed, Atum floated as a substance containing the seeds of life in a primaeval watery expanse called Nun. He emerged, self-created, standing on a mound called the *benben*. The ancient Egyptians took this image from the mounds of fertile silt that emerged from the waters of the Nile once the annual flood began to subside. Atum then created the first couple, Shu and Tefnut.

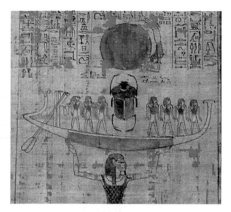

Every night Atum journeys through the Underworld, executing enemies and over-throwing the gigantic serpent called Apophis. Atum had a number of sacred creatures including the lion, mongoose and snake.

A picture from a papyrus showing the god Nun raising the solar boat containing forms of the sun-god above the primaeval water.

# KHEPRY

Khepry is another name for the sun-god in his form as a scarab beetle. He takes this form as he leaves the Underworld to rise over the eastern horizon at dawn.

In daily life the ancient Egyptians often saw scarab beetles rolling balls of dung across the ground. Consequently, they imagined that a gigantic scarab beetle pushed the sun into the sky. Also, they noticed newly-hatched scarab beetles crawling out of dung balls in which the eggs had been laid. It looked as if the beetles had come into existence from nothing. This reminded the Egyptians of the way in which the creator sun-god emerged from the primaeval waters. The name Khepry means the 'Self-developing One.'

In the funerary cult, a scarab inscribed with a spell in hieroglyphs was placed over the heart of the mummy.

A cloisonné pectoral showing Khepry propelling the sun-disc.

Temple priests sometimes placed colossal stone scarabs like this one beside the sacred lakes in the temple precinct.

6

# RE

The sun-god Re in his form of Re-Horakhty is a hawk, crowned with the sun-disc circled by the cobra-goddess Wadjyt.

Re-Horakhty combines the image of the sun as a fiery disc with the majesty of a hawk soaring high in the sky. The name Horakhty asserts the hawk-god as ruler over both the eastern and western horizons.

The ancient Egyptians wrote many hymns to Re-Horakhty. The most important one begins the Book of the Dead, a collection of spells to guide the dead safely to the afterlife. The hymn praises the god as he rises at dawn. In some of the surviving papyrus scrolls of the Book of the Dead, beautiful vignettes (pictures) accompany this hymn.

Re-Horakhty with baboons, who are sacred to Egyptian moon-gods. The baboons are screeching and waving their paws at the sun-god in joy at his rising and in recognition of his sovereignty.

# SHU & TEFNUT

Shu is the air-god. In one ancient Egyptian myth, the creator sun-god sneezed out Shu, whose name has a similar sound to the verb 'to sneeze' in ancient Egyptian (roughly pronounced 'asheshesh').

The sun-god spat out the goddess Tefnut. Her name partly resembles the ancient Egyptian word *tef* meaning 'to spit'. Tefnut is a goddess not easy to define but she may personify the moisture in the atmosphere or the morning dew. She may even be the air-goddess of the Underworld.

Shu physically separates earth and sky by holding the body of the sky-goddess Nut high above that of her husband, the earth-god Geb.

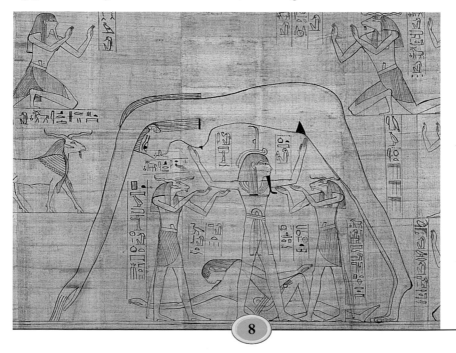

# GEB & NUT

This couple are the children of Shu and Tefnut and their roles complete the physical geography of the ancient Egyptian universe.

Geb is the earth-god. The Nile Valley stretches along his body. He is represented as a man, lying down and leaning on one arm. Often his skin is green to indicate vegetation and the fertility of the land of Egypt. For example, barley, ancient Egypt's staple crop for bread, sprouted from his ribs. His name is written with the hieroglyph of a goose, which he sometimes wears as an emblem on his head.

Nut is the sky-goddess who arches her body over Geb with her hands and feet resting on the four cardinal points north, south, east and west (see page 8). Less frequently she takes the shape of a celestial cow. Nut's body is a barrier that prevents chaotic and destructive forces in the universe crashing down onto Egypt. In the Underworld Nut is the goddess of the sycamore fig tree and is depicted rising from its trunk to provide air, water and nourishment eternally.

The children of Geb and Nut are the deities Osiris, Seth, Isis and Nephthys, all of whom figure in the myth of kingship.

Nut is often represented on the inside of coffin lids.

# PTAH

Ptah is the creator god of Memphis, the capital city of Egypt founded by the first pharaoh around 3000 BC. One ancient Egyptian name for Memphis was 'Enclosure of the spirit of Ptah'.

Ptah has the form of a human man, tightly wrapped in a robe. Ptah is the patron god of craftsmen, builders, and sculptors and he is responsible for creative thought and the magical force of words. His wife is the lioness-goddess Sekhmet.

An inscription on a granite slab describes how Ptah created the world. Ptah was alone on the mound that had arisen from the primaeval water. He thought in his heart about everything that he felt ought to exist. Then he spoke it into existence with a command that produced all the forces and elements present in the world, including the other gods and the land of Egypt.

Ptah wears a close-fitting cap and holds a complex sceptre with the symbols for life, stability and dominion.

Ptah with a worshipper. Behind the god are ears, showing that he is listening to his worshipper's prayer.

*See also Sekhmet page 15*

# THE APIS BULL

The Apis bull is the sacred creature of Ptah, worshipped as his 'living image'.

Priests had to find a special bull that was black with a white triangle on its forehead. Its tail hairs had to divide into two distinct strands. The priests were supposed to find a scarab beetle under its tongue. The Apis bull lived in palatial quarters in the temple of Ptah and at festivals would be seen at the 'Window of Appearances' just like a pharaoh. One of the rituals in the royal jubilee festival was for the pharaoh to stride along beside the Apis to prove his vigour had not grown less. When Apis died it was mummified then taken with great ceremony to the necropolis (cemetery) of Memphis. The bull mummy was buried in a vast sarcophagus (coffin) in an underground catacomb.

A bronze figurine of the Apis bull. He carries a sun-disc between his horns on which is Wadjyt, the cobra-goddess, and his back is decorated with the wings of the vulture-goddess Nekhbet.

*See also The Two Ladies pages 18-19*

# KHNUM

The creator god Khnum is usually shown as a man with the head of a ram.

Khnum creates everything in the universe on his potter's wheel. He shapes all the other gods, the human race (foreigners and Egyptians alike), animals, birds, fish and reptiles – one of his titles is 'Lord of the Crocodiles'.

Khnum is closely connected to the River Nile, which was the lifeblood of ancient Egypt. It was at Khnum's command that the god Hapy caused the annual Nile inundation, which brought with it the fertile silt crucial to farmers. Once, Khnum prevented the flood for seven years, causing severe famine in Egypt. He only relented once the pharaoh promised to donate to him gold and luxury goods from Nubia. There was a major temple to Khnum on the island of Elephantine at Aswan and mummified sacred rams were buried there.

A finely carved relief of Khnum.

See also Hapy page 42

# BASTET

The cat-goddess Bastet is the daughter of Re, the sun-god. Originally she was a lioness and could inspire terror.

She also protects royalty. About 1000 BC her image changed and she was more frequently represented as the cat, who destroys vermin but is friendly to people.

Bastet's main cult centre was in the Egyptian Delta at Bubastis. Today massive fallen red-granite blocks mark the site of the temple. Nearly 2500 years ago a famous Greek writer called Herodotus visited Bubastis during the festival of Bastet. He describes how everyone arrived in barges singing, playing pipes or shaking clappers and drinking wine.

Sacred cats lived in Bastet's temple. When they died, they were mummified and wrapped in linen with often a rather surprised look painted on their faces. A bronze mask was placed over their heads, they were put into a coffin in the shape of a seated cat and buried in the temple cemetery.

Thousands of votive bronzes of Bastet as a stately, seated cat or as a woman with a cat's head were made and dedicated at her temple.

# HATHOR

Hathor as a woman with cow's ears, shown on the prow of the ceremonial boat of an Egyptian queen.

Hathor is one of the most ancient and important goddesses. Sometimes she appears as a cow carrying between her horns the disk of her father, the sun-god Re. Sometimes she is a beautiful woman with the ears of a cow, or wearing a headdress of cow horns and a sun-disc.

Hathor is the goddess of love and often features in Egyptian love poems. She is also the goddess of joy, music and dancing. Her priestesses celebrated her by shaking a ritual rattle known as a *sistrum* and a sacred necklace called a *menat*. Once she even cheered up the sun-god, who was sulking, by striking a saucy pose in front of him! Hathor is also the guardian of the necropolis (the burial place), particularly at Thebes during the New Kingdom. In royal tombs she is shown in the burial chamber, protecting the monarch. Queens of Egypt often showed themselves in art looking like Hathor, as Queen Nefertari did in her famous temple at Abu Simbel.

In the Books of the Dead, papyri placed in the tombs of noble Egyptians, Hathor is shown as a cow. She is coming from the desert into the papyrus marshes, linking the necropolis with the land of living Egypt.

# SEKHMET

Lioness-headed Sekhmet is the daughter of Re, the sun-god, and the wife of Ptah.

In one myth, ferocious Sekhmet almost wiped out the human race. The sun-god felt that humans were plotting against him so he sent his daughter to punish them. Sekhmet slaughtered so many people that Re was afraid that no-one would be left to look after the temples and make offerings. So he poured out a lake of beer and coloured it with red ochre, to look like blood. Next day Sekhmet found what she thought was a lake of blood left over from the killing. She drank it, became intoxicated and wandered away happy, so humanity was saved.

Because Sekhmet was so fierce, the Egyptians thought that she might be able to fight off plagues and cure diseases for which doctors had no remedies.

Hundreds of statues of Sekhmet, standing or seated, were set up in Theban temples as part of a ritual that celebrated her father Re, the sun-god.

15

*See also Ptah, page 10*

# NEITH

Neith is a goddess of great antiquity with a complex role in Egyptian religion.

Her trademarks are weapons of war, either a shield with arrows crossing it or two bows bound together. These symbols led early Greek visitors to Egypt to identify Neith with their own warlike goddess Athene. But Neith is a creator goddess as well. She emerged from the primaeval water in Upper Egypt and glided north to the western Nile Delta to found her sanctuary at Sais. Neith is also one of the goddesses presiding over the conception and birth of the pharaoh. Neith extends her protection to the monarch and elite into the afterlife. She is one of the four goddesses who guards the Canopic chest containing the embalmed inner organs of the mummified person.

Her relationship with the god Seth resulted in her giving birth to the crocodile-god Sobek.

Neith is often depicted as a woman wearing the Red Crown of Lower Egypt.

16

See also Seth page 30, Sobek page 43

# SELQET

The scorpion-goddess Selqet is naturally a guardian deity and is also important in spells to cure poisonous bites and stings.

Selqet is often shown as a woman with the scorpion ready to sting on her head. Sometimes the scorpion is shown without the lethal part of its poisonous tail, in case it should magically come to life. Her name in full is Selqet-hetet, which means 'She who lets the throat breathe'. This might refer to the hope of everyone that a scorpion sting will not threaten their life – or more ominously it might refer to the deep panic gasps for breath caused by a scorpion sting. The 'Priests of Selqet' were medico-magicians specializing in cures for scorpion and snake bites.

A gilded statuette of Selqet from the tomb of Tutankhamun. She guarded the Canopic chest containing his mummified organs. The scorpion on her head has no sting.

# THE TWO LADIES

The Two Ladies, Wadjyt and Nekhbet, are fierce goddesses who protect the sun-god and the pharaoh.

On this bracelet Wadjyt, in her cobra form, protects the sun-god.

Nekhbet is a vulture-goddess who is often shown as a vulture with her wings outspread and dipped at the tips, holding in her claws the ring-shapes symbolizing 'eternity'. Nekhbet is protectress of the monarch's power in Upper Egypt and she often wears the White Crown of the south. Nekhbet's image can be seen in the official titles of the pharaoh and sometimes on the royal headdress.

Wadjyt is the cobra-goddess who appears as a rearing snake. She sometimes combines with her southern counterpart Nekhbet, and has vulture wings and talons coming from her serpent coils. Wadjyt's name comes from the Egyptian word meaning 'to be green', in the sense of flourishing like the papyrus marshes. The symbol above all others that marked out royalty in ancient Egypt was the cobra-goddess worn on the crown or forehead of the pharaoh. Wadjyt, rising up ready to spit fire at all enemies of the king, was described by the Greeks as the Uraeus.

Wadjyt is also sometimes shown as a lioness, especially in her role as the 'Eye of Re', one of the terrifying daughters of the sun-god who slaughtered his enemies.

The Two Ladies, Nekhbet and Wadjyt, painted on a coffin.

# AMUN

Amun, who combines with the sun-god to become Amun-Re, is the King of the Gods.

The Egyptians saw all the other major gods as a series of manifestations of Amun. His huge temple at Karnak was continually embellished by pharaohs for over 2,000 years and pharaohs claimed Amun was their father. Amun's name means the 'Hidden One' and his true nature is totally secret. Amun is also the god of military expansion. He holds the scimitar of war out to the pharaoh to conquer foreign territory. During the Middle Eastern campaign of Rameses the Great (reigning from 1270 BC) Amun's intervention allegedly saved the pharaoh from being killed by Hittite troops. At the other end of the social hierarchy, Amun protected poor people in law courts from corrupt judges.

A statue of the pharaoh Taharqo with Amun in the form of his sacred animal, the ram.

A gold and silver statuette of Amun. He is often shown in human form with a crown of two tall plumes.

# MUT

Mut is the most important goddess of Thebes and is the chief consort of Amun.

Her name is written with the hieroglyph of a vulture and her appearance is that of a human woman wearing a vulture headdress surmounted by the Double Crown of Upper and Lower Egypt.

Mut had her own sanctuary just south of the temple of Amun at Karnak. It was linked to the main temple by a processional road passing through imposing towering gateways or pylons. Mut is also a lioness-goddess and a cat-goddess. Hundreds of granite statues of the lioness-deity Sekhmet were dedicated in Mut's temple, emphasizing the close relationship between these two major goddesses.

The goddess Mut.

*See also Sekhmet page 15*

# KHONSU

The moon-god Khonsu was worshipped at Thebes as the child of Amun and Mut.

His name means 'wanderer', describing the path of the moon across the sky. He can appear in a number of forms: as a child, as a hawk-headed god or as a baboon, the moon's sacred animal. In all cases he can have the crown combining the crescent and full moon.

Khonsu has a temple at Karnak at the beginning of the processional road to the New Year Festival Temple of Luxor. His statues were renowned for their healing powers. A tale invented by his priests describes how one statue of Khonsu was sent on a seventeen-month journey to a remote country called Bakhtan to cure Princess Bentresh, who was possessed by an evil spirit.

A bronze figurine of Khonsu as a child. He wears his hair in a side-lock, a hairstyle worn only by children in ancient Egypt.

# ATEN

Aten is the most abstract form of the sun-god. He is shown as the solar disc whose rays end in hands, some of which extend the hieroglyph for 'life' to the royal family.

Aten became the supreme god in the Egyptian pantheon for less than twenty years in the reign of the pharaoh Akhenaten (1352-1336 BC).

Akhenaten tried to establish the cult of Aten at Thebes, overthrowing the long-established authority of Amun, but the priests resisted him. He then decided to found a completely new city for Aten at a site he called 'Akhet-Aten', meaning the 'Horizon of the Sun-disc' (today known as El-Amarna). Akhenaten wrote a magnificent hymn to Aten stressing that Aten was the sole creator god, responsible for all life-forms in the universe. After Akhenaten's death, his ideas were rejected and his reign became regarded as a disaster for Egypt.

The pharaoh Akhenaten with the rays of the sun-disc. Akhenaten emphasized that only he and his Queen Nefertiti could address prayers directly to his 'father' Aten.

23

See also Amun, page 20

# MONTU

Montu is a warrior god. He held a prominent position in the region of Thebes but he became less important when the god Amun came on the scene.

Still, his four major sanctuaries flourished for 2000 years. Montu is shown as a hawk-headed god wearing a crown of plumes and a solar disc encircled by two images of the cobra-goddess Wadjyt. On military campaigns pharaohs such as Thutmose III (1479-1425 BC) were described as being like Montu in his glittering war chariot. Montu's cult involved the worship of a sacred bull called Buchis. The necropolis for these bulls has been discovered in the desert near Montu's principal temple at Armant, just south of Luxor.

Montu (in the centre) with his crown of plumes.

# ISIS

Isis is a goddess with great magical powers. Her name is written with the hieroglyph of a throne, which she can wear on her head as well as the crown of cow horns and sun-disc.

Isis married her brother Osiris and they had a son, Horus. Osiris was murdered by Seth, who stole his throne. Isis outwitted Seth with her magic and the throne of Egypt was given to Horus. The pharaoh identifies with Horus, so Isis is symbolically his divine mother. Isis had to use magic to protect Horus against dangers when he was a child, so she was invoked by Egyptian women when their own children were sick with fevers or bitten by poisonous animals. Isis became 'great in magic' because the sun-god revealed to her his secret name – knowledge that gave her unique power. She made a serpent out of clay mixed with the saliva of the sun-god and caused it to bite him. Then she refused to heal his pain until he revealed the name. Eventually the cult of Isis spread from Egypt across Europe. Isis was the last Egyptian goddess to be worshipped before Christianity finally suppressed all other cults.

A statue of Isis protecting her husband Osiris.

25

See also Osiris pages 34-35

# NEPHTHYS

Like her sister Isis, Nephthys is the daughter of Geb and Nut. Her name can be translated as 'Mistress of the Enclosure'.

She had a liaison with her brother Seth and also a brief love affair with Osiris which resulted in her giving birth to the jackal-god Anubis.

Nephthys is of immense support to Isis after the murder of their brother Osiris. Together they lament his death and perform the magic to bring him back to life so that Isis can conceive her son Horus.

Nephthys is often shown carved on stone sarcophagi (coffins), kneeling by the head of the deceased person or protecting the Canopic chest.

A figurine of weeping Nephthys, mourning the death of Osiris.

Opposite: Isis and her sister Nephthys.

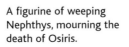

27

*See also Anubis page 36*

# HORUS

The hawk-god Horus is the manifestation of divine kingship.

The title 'Horus', first used on royal monuments five thousand years ago, is the earliest way of describing the pharaoh. The wife of Horus is the goddess Hathor. In another tradition, Horus is a sun-god depicted in many tombs and temples as a solar disc with a hawk's wings.

Horus is the child of Osiris and Isis and in his early years is vulnerable to attacks by the usurper Seth. After an 80-year struggle, he becomes the rightful ruler of Egypt. In one episode in the violent conflict, Seth cuts out the eyes of Horus but these are restored by the magic of the goddess Hathor. The 'Eye of Horus' is a powerful amulet. Known as the Wadjet Eye, it stands for soundness and perfection and protects everything, which is why it is so common in jewellery, on coffins or on Nile boats. The best-preserved temple in Egypt at Edfu is dedicated to Horus. It actually has a sacred play carved on its walls celebrating the triumph of Horus over Seth in the form of a hippopotamus. The hippo-Seth is harpooned and then cut to pieces.

Horus, shown as a Roman legionary.

The infant Horus shown triumphing over dangerous creatures, including scorpions and snakes.

# SETH

Seth is an exciting, unpredictable god. He has great strength, but he appears in a bad light in the myth of his brother Osiris.

Seth is shown as a mythical animal – a four-footed creature with a curved beak, two upright ears and a forked tail.

Seth was venerated as a major god of royalty from the beginning of pharaonic civilization, five thousand years ago, to at least 1000 BC. In battle he gives his strength to Rameses the Great to overcome the Hittites.

Seth is the arch-villain in the struggle to be ruler of Egypt. He murders Osiris and takes the throne from Horus, leading to a long and sometimes violent power-struggle. Eventually even Seth's most powerful supporter, the sun-god, has to concede that Horus is the winner. As a consolation prize Seth is given two Middle Eastern goddesses as wives. Re also adopts Seth to act as thunder in the sky and to travel with the sun-god through the underworld to use his strength against the serpent Apophis.

The Seth animal carved above the names of the pharaoh Peribsen. During Peribsen's reign Seth briefly took the place of Horus as the dynastic god.

# PHARAOH

A stela showing Amenhotep I and Ahmose Nefertari worshipped as gods.

In ancient Egypt the pharaoh was divine, the earthly manifestation of the god Horus.

He was also given the title 'Son of Re', linking him to the all-powerful sun-god. At the pharaoh's coronation the gods Horus and Thoth ritually purified him with a bath of the hieroglyphs for 'life' and 'dominion'.

After a reign of thirty years the pharaoh celebrated his *heb-sed* or jubilee festival. He rejuvenated his physical prowess with rituals including firing arrows to the cardinal points (north, south, east and west) to assert his universal rule.

Some monarchs were especially revered for centuries after their deaths, such as Amenhotep I and his mother Ahmose-Nefertari. They gave 500 years of employment to craftsmen, stone-masons and labourers by founding a village just for the workers on the tombs in the Valley of the Kings. Other rulers were damned to oblivion after they died by being left out of the King Lists set up in temples. One of these was Queen Hatshepsut, who defied convention and ruled as if she were a male pharaoh.

This granite statue of Rameses shows the king's divine regalia: a head-cloth with the symbol of the cobra-goddess Wadjyt, the ceremonial straight false beard, and the crook and flail sceptres.

# WEPWAWET

Wepwawet is a jackal-god of Upper Egypt. He first appears on early Egyptian battle standards that were paraded before the ruler to celebrate a military triumph.

Wepwawet's name means 'Opener of the Ways' and suits a god who goes before the pharaoh on military campaigns to extend the frontiers of Egypt. Wepwawet is also the 'Opener of the Ways' for the dead through the perils of the Underworld. In a ritual drama performed at Abydos concerning Osiris, Wepwawet fends off attacks on the god's boat in the procession by enemies symbolizing supporters of Seth.

An Early Dynastic ivory label which has the inscription 'The first occasion of smiting the Easterners'. In front of the standard of Wepwawet is a billowing object known as the *shedshed* which helps the pharaoh ascend into the sky in the Hereafter.

# UNDERWORLD DEITIES

The ferocious Underworld Deities have to be passed by each dead person on their way to reach Osiris in the Underworld.

The papyrus scroll called in ancient Egypt the 'Book of going forth by day', and in modern times the 'Book of the Dead', contains pictures and spells to help a dead person get past all perils. These dangers include the twelve caverns where gods and goddesses behead the enemies of the sun-god and eat their corpses and souls. Similarly there are seven gates for seven gods through which everyone has to pass. Each one is guarded by a keeper and a herald armed with knives. The spells give the dead person power over these threatening beings by telling their secret names (some frightening like 'Hippopotamus Face' and some revolting like 'Maggot-eater') so that they will allow the person through. The dead person then has the same magical spells to get him or her through twenty-one secret doorways in the mansion of Osiris himself.

One of the Underworld Deities.

# OSIRIS

Osiris is the ruler of the Underworld. He was king of Egypt until Seth murdered him and cut his body into fourteen pieces, scattering them throughout Egypt.

His wife Isis 'great in magic' founded a temple to Osiris wherever she came across a bit of his body. His major cult centre at Abydos in Upper Egypt is where she found his head. Once Isis and Horus were set to avenge his death, Osiris left Egypt to become the king of the Underworld. His title 'Foremost of the Westerners' indicates his importance in the region where the sun set — that is, where the sun-god descended into the realm of the dead. Usually Osiris is shown tightly wrapped in linen bandages like a mummy.

Osiris' skin is often shown as black or green, both very positive colours in ancient Egypt symbolizing fertility and life.

34

*See also Isis pages 25-26*

Osiris frequently holds his special symbol, called the *djed*-pillar, which stands for the backbone of Osiris. In the Underworld Osiris is the judge of the dead. He is ready to punish any evildoers but offers eternity to those who have led reasonable lives.

Osiris holds the crook and flail sceptres of a pharaoh and wears the distinctive *atef* crown – a tall cone decorated with ostrich plumes and ram's horns.

# ANUBIS

Anubis is the jackal god who supervizes mummification and guards the desert cemeteries.

He can appear as a man with a jackal's head or as a crouching jackal wearing a magical collar. Although jackals normally have tawny hides, Anubis is black. The colour represents the fertile soil in which crops grow each year and suggests being born again in the next life. Egyptians saw Anubis as the embalmer of Osiris and of the pharaohs – and in real life a priest wearing a jackal mask was present for mummification rituals. After the organs were removed from the body, Anubis purified it with precious oils and unguents. He also washed the removed internal organs and kept them safe. At the time of burial a priest wearing a jackal mask took part in the 'Opening the Mouth' ceremony (a ritual to restore living faculties to the deceased). He touched the mouth of the mummy-case with an adze made of iron brought down from the sky by Anubis.

Anubis took part in the 'Weighing of the Heart' ceremony to judge whether a dead person could be admitted to the afterlife.

# THE SONS OF HORUS

During mummification the internal organs (except for the heart) were removed to stop them rotting inside the body.

The organs were not thrown away in case they fell into the possession of some-one intent on working an evil spell against the deceased's spirit. The organs were wrapped in linen packages and put into the four Canopic jars. Each jar had a stopper in the shape of a protecting god. Collectively these gods are known as the Sons of Horus. The human-headed god is Imsety who looks after the liver, the baboon is Hapy, who protects the lungs, the jackal is Duamutef, who guards the stomach and the hawk is Qebehsenuef, who defends the intestines. The jars were placed in a Canopic chest, which was watched over by four great goddesses: Isis, Nephthys, Neith and Selqet.

Canopic jars with the heads of the Sons of Horus.

# ASSESSOR GODS

Every dead person has to enter the Broad Hall of the Two Truths to be judged.

The dead person's heart is weighed in a pair of scales against Maat, the goddess of Truth. She has the form of a woman with an ostrich feather on her head or sometimes just the feather. Anubis checks the scales while Thoth as a baboon sometimes sits on top in his role as god of accuracy. Forty-two Assessor Gods – one for each district of Upper and Lower Egypt – now interrogate the deceased about their past life. Each god is named, sometimes in a way to inspire terror such as 'Bone-breaker' or 'Blood-drinker'. The Book of the Dead provides the right answers to these questions. No lies can be told in the presence of Maat. If the person comes out well from this examination, Thoth declares them 'True of Voice' and they are then led by Horus into the realm of Osiris. Otherwise their hopes for paradise will be crushed in the jaws of the goddess Ammut.

Three Assessor Gods.

# AMMUT

Ammut is a dreaded Underworld goddess who prominently figures in the 'Weighing of the Heart' ceremony.

She is ferocious to look at, with a crocodile head, a lion or leopard body and the hind legs of a hippopotamus. Her name means 'Devourer of the Dead'.

If a dead person is judged to be guilty by the Assessor Gods, then the person's heart is thrown to Ammut. She will eat it up, thereby destroying any hope of an afterlife for the deceased. Egyptian 'Weighing of the Heart' scenes always show this goddess, who constitutes the ultimate threat to eternal life, but she is of course always left hungry.

Ammut waits beside Thoth for a heart to be weighed.

*See also Thoth page 45*

# APOPHIS

Apophis is the Underworld snake that threatens the very existence of the sun-god.

Apophis's coils are 16 metres (nearly 50 feet) long. When the sun-god and his entourage descend in his boat below the western mountains into the Underworld, Apophis mesmerizes all with a stare. But this potential catastrophe is averted by Seth who enchants Apophis with a spell.

Even if Apophis has no victims to devour, he can survive by breathing in his own ear-splitting roars. Although Apophis can never be permanently destroyed, images show him being temporarily killed to enable the sun-god to pass safely to another region of the Underworld. So he is described as being hacked-up and burnt and is shown with spears in his coils, chained by his neck or being decapitated.

The great cat of Re beheads Apophis.

# 𓇓𓏏𓊪 BES

Bes is an ugly god but all his powers are on the side of the family.

He is a bandy-legged dwarf with some of the features of a lion. He often wears a panther skin and holds a weapon to show he is ready to defend a woman and her newly-born children.

One of his responsibilities in a temple is to ensure that the child of the major god and goddess is symbolically born without problems. The part of the temple-enclosure where this protection was guaranteed is called the Birth-House or Mammisi.

Bes often appears as a decoration on headrests, footboards, cosmetic containers or mirrors. He is also a god who enjoys music, particularly the tambourine or lute.

Bes has an important role as a god who will prevent snakes and scorpions harming the family.

Bes has lion's ears and his facial features are leonine. Here he is accompanied by a monkey.

# HAPY

Hapy is the god of the annual Nile inundation (flood).

The beginning of the ancient Egyptian New Year was marked by a rise in the level of the River Nile, which flooded the fields with water and with fertile silt. Hapy's body takes the form of a corpulent male with pendulous breasts, symbolizing agricultural prosperity resulting from the flood. Frequently he wears a headdress of lotus or papyrus plants.

Hapy was thought to live in a cavern under the First Nile Cataract just south of Aswan. No temples were dedicated to him but he is shown in statues and on wall reliefs, and hymns were sung to him. Sometimes the pharaoh is shown as Hapy.

A statue of the pharaoh Horemheb playing the role of the god Hapy, with an offering-table of lotuses and other Nile plants.

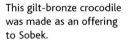 # SOBEK

Sobek is the crocodile-god. In ancient Egypt crocodiles lurked on the banks of the Nile or in the marshes, intent on snatching and eating people or cattle.

Sobek's lethal strength led to his association with the supposedly all-powerful pharaoh. Sobek's mother was the goddess Neith.

Sobek was worshipped at Kom-Ombo in Upper Egypt, where there was an extensive cemetery for mummified crocodiles. He was also a principal god among the Greek and Roman settlers in the Faiyum area of Egypt.

Priests of Sobek had the tricky job of adorning living sacred crocodiles with jewellery.

This gilt-bronze crocodile was made as an offering to Sobek.

43

*See also Neith page 16*

# TAWERET

This goddess looks dangerous, having a snarling hippopotamus head, the body of a pregnant woman, the arms and legs of a lion and a crocodile tail.

However, all her ferocity is meant to ward off any threats to women during childbirth and she often holds the powerful amulet of protection.

Taweret's headdress has cow horns and a sun-disc with plumes, like other goddesses who were protectors of women and children, such as Hathor. Taweret's name means 'The Great One' or 'The Big One'. Sometimes she is represented in large, impressive statues but more often she takes the form of a small amulet with a suspension loop worn by women on bracelets or necklaces. In the ancient Egyptian signs of the zodiac Taweret forms one of the constellations of the northern sky.

A large breccia statue of Taweret which came from a temple.

44

*See also Hathor page 14*

# THOTH

Thoth in his ibis-headed form. In the 'Weighing of the Heart' ceremony he announces to Osiris that the deceased deserves eternal life.

Thoth is the god of all knowledge and can appear either as an ibis or a baboon.

He is also the moon-god and wears the combined crescent and full moons as a crown. Both Thoth's sacred creatures can suggest lunar symbolism – the curved beak of the ibis is the moon's crescent, and baboons become agitated at the end of the night. 'Thoth' is the Greek version of his name. The hieroglyphs of his name actually spell out 'Djhwty', which in English we would pronounce as 'Djeheuty'. Thoth gave the 'god's words' – the ancient Egyptian term for hieroglyphs – to humankind on the instructions of the sun-god. The scribes recognized the magical power of these signs. Only the elite were allowed to learn to read and write hieroglyphs.

Thoth's main cult centre was at Hermopolis (modern Ashmunein) where he was at the head of eight primaeval creator deities. There were extensive underground catacombs for mummified ibises and baboons in the nearby desert necropolis (cemetery).

Thoth in his baboon form, wearing his moon headdress.

45

# MAAT

Maat is the goddess of truth, and a daughter of the creator sun-god. She is shown as a beautiful woman wearing on her head the ostrich feather that is the hieroglyph of her name.

Maat is extremely important because she personifies the ordered structure of the universe and opposes the forces of chaos. Consequently the pharaohs of Egypt are shown in every major temple holding up an effigy of Maat to indicate that their rule is based upon the principles that she stands for. In the afterlife, the dead have their hearts weighed against Maat in her role as goddess of truth to see if they have lived lives sufficiently blameless to enter the realm of Osiris. Sometimes Egyptian judges wore pendants of Maat in the law courts to show that their decisions were honest and unbiased.

A gold pendant in the shape of the goddess Maat.

# IMHOTEP

Imhotep was a very high official of King Djoser in about 2660 BC.

Imhotep was also a master sculptor and planned the first huge stone monument in the world, the king's Step Pyramid at Saqqara. One of the pieces of proof of Imhotep's historical existence is an inscription on the base of a statue of the king that gives the name of Imhotep. This was an exceptionally rare privilege.

After Imhotep's death his fame continued to grow. He was credited as the author of a Book of Wisdom, which unfortunately has not survived. Scribes looked to him as a kind of patron saint. Eventually the memory of his architectural skills led to him being seen as the son of Ptah of Memphis, a god particularly associated with craftsmen.

Imhotep was worshipped as a god at Saqqara, Thebes and in the temple of Isis on the island of Philae. He acquired a reputation as a god of healing, and early Greek visitors to Egypt identified him with their own god of medicine, Asklepios.

Statuettes of Imhotep show him seated, with a papyrus scroll on his lap, wearing a tight-fitting cap.

See also Ptah page 10

# SARAPIS

In 305 BC Egypt was conquered by a Macedonian Greek called Alexander the Great.

After Alexander's death his general, Ptolemy, became pharaoh of Egypt. He began the Ptolemaic dynasty which lasted nearly 300 years, ending in 30 BC when Queen Cleopatra VII committed suicide.

As a Greek ruler of Egypt, Ptolemy wanted to combine Egyptian and Greek religious ideas in one god. So Sarapis was invented. From the Egyptian side Sarapis was made up from the cult of Osiris, ruler of the Underworld, also connected with agricultural prosperity, and Apis, the sacred bull of the god Ptah of Memphis. The god's name derives from Osiris–Apis. From the Greek pantheon Sarapis takes elements from Zeus, the king of the gods, from Helios, the sun-god, from Hades, god of the Underworld, from Dionysos, god of fertility in nature and from Asklepios, god of healing. There were hardly any temples to Sarapis in Egypt, except in Ptolemy's capital Alexandria, but many sanctuaries to him were built throughout the Mediterranean world – such as on the island of Delos – where he was shown together with his consort Isis.

Sarapis is shown as a Greek god with flowing locks of hair and a full beard, wearing a corn-measure on his head.

48

*See also Osiris pages 34-35, Apis Bull page 11*